HORRIBLE HABITATS

Rotten Logs and Forest Floors

Sharon Katz Cooper

Chicago, Illinois

www.heinemannraintree.com
Visit our website to find out
more information about
Heinemann-Raintree books.

To order:

☎ Phone 888-454-2279

💻 Visit www.heinemannraintree.com
to browse our catalog and order online.

© 2010 Raintree
an imprint of Capstone Global Library, LLC
Chicago, Illinois

Edited by Charlotte Guillain, Rebecca Rissman, and
Sian Smith
Designed by Joanna Hinton-Malivoire
Picture research by Tracy Cummins and
Heather Mauldin
Originated by Chroma Graphics (Overseas) Pte. Ltd
Printed and bound in China by Leo Paper Products

14 13 12 11 10
10 9 8 7 6 5 4 3 2 1

**Library of Congress Cataloging-in-Publication
Data**
Katz Cooper, Sharon.
Rotten logs and forest floors / Sharon Katz Cooper.
p. cm. -- (Horrible habitats)
Includes bibliographical references and index.
ISBN 978-1-4109-3493-2 (hc)
ISBN 978-1-4109-3501-4 (pb)
1. Forest animals--Habitat--Juvenile literature. 2. Dead
trees--Ecology--Juvenile literature. 3. Forest litter--
Biodegradation--Juvenile literature. I. Title.
QL112.K373 2009
591.73--dc22
                                    2009002605

Acknowledgments
The author and publisher are grateful to the following
for permission to reproduce copyright material:
Age Fotostock p. **10** (© Joel Sartore); Alamy pp. **6**
(© Chuck Place), **17** (© Scott Camazine), **20** (© Arco
Images/Muehlmann, K.), **22** (© Nature Picture Library/
Jose B. Ruiz), **23** (© Bruce Coleman Inc./John Bell);
Bugwood.org p. **26** (© Scott Bauer, USDA Agricultural
Research Service); Dwight Kuhn Photography p. **19**
(© Dwight Kuhn); Getty Images p. **12** (© Bill Beatty);
Minden p. **11** (© Mark Moffett); Nature Picture
Library p. **14** (© Adrian Davies); Photolibrary pp. **8** (©
Science Photo Library), **18** (© Oxford Scientific), **25** (©
Michael Fogden); Shutterstock pp. **4** (© Kirsanov), **5**
(© letty17), **7** (© Aleksander Bolbot), **9**, **13** (© Joseph
Calev), **15** (© Neale Cousland), **21** (© Gert Johannes
Jacobus Vrey), **29** background (© Vojta Herout), **29a**
(© Nicholas Piccillo), **29b** (© Graham Taylor), **29c** (©
Pakhnyushcha), **29d** (© Babusi Octavian Florentin),
29e (© Ljupco Smokovski), **29f** (© pixelman); Visuals
Unlimited, Inc. pp. **16** (© Steve Strickland), **24** (© Dr.
Dennis Kunkel), **27** (© Dr. Dennis Kunkel).

Cover photograph of an earthworm reproduced with
permission of Photo Researchers, Inc. (© Wayne G.
Lawler).

Every effort has been made to contact copyright
holders of any material reproduced in this book. Any
omissions will be rectified in subsequent printings if
notice is given to the publisher.

Some words are shown in bold, **like this**. You can find
out what they mean by looking in the glossary.

Contents

What Is a Habitat?

A **habitat** is a place where animals can get the things they need to live. Just like you, they need food, water, and shelter.

frog

newly fallen tree

rotting tree

Can you spot the differences between this rotting tree and the tree that has just fallen?

A tree falls in the forest. Crash! But that is not the end of the tree's story. It's just the beginning of its new life as a rotting **habitat**.

Who's on Your Back?

Rotting logs are full of creatures so tiny you can't see them. These are called **microbes**. They often ride into the log on an ant's body.

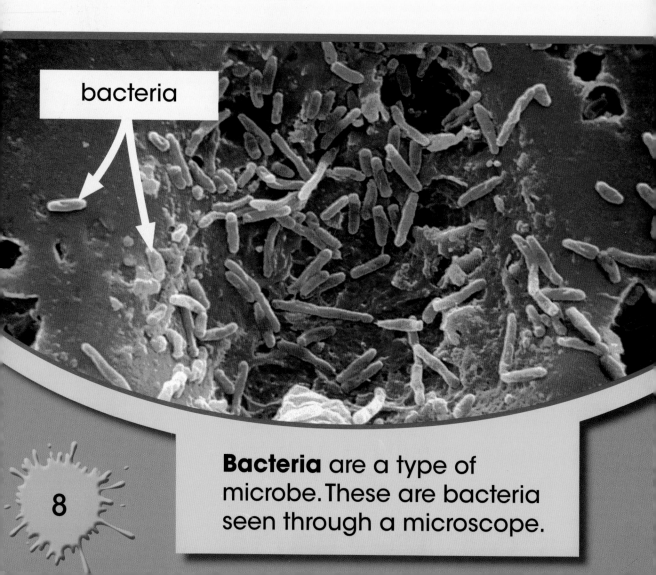

bacteria

Bacteria are a type of microbe. These are bacteria seen through a microscope.

FUN FACT

Bacteria living on ants make **antibiotics**. These antibiotics help stop ants and their babies from getting sick.

Slurp and Burp!

Bess beetles use **microbes** in their guts to **digest**, or break down, rotting wood. Baby beetles do not have these microbes. To get them, they call to an adult beetle. The adult beetle vomits food with microbes into the baby's mouth.

larva

adult beetle

This photo shows adult beetles and a baby beetle, or **larva**.

11

Have you ever seen a pill bug? They like to eat anything that is rotting. On the forest floor, they eat rotting leaves and wood.

pill bug

FUN FACT

Pill bugs are not insects. They are related to lobsters and crabs!

new shell

old shell

As pill bugs grow, they lose their old shells and grow new ones. This is called **molting**.

13

Once a log gets soft from holes and water, new creatures come to eat. They come to eat the wood-eaters and their poo. Some even eat the **microbes** growing on poo. Yum!

soft, wet wood

fungus

Some insects plant a **fungus** garden on their log. Fungus is like mold or mushrooms. The insects plant a tiny bit of fungus on the log. When the fungus grows, they eat it!

Here Come the Ants!

Some ants love rotting logs. They don't eat wood. They dig through it to make a shelter. Inside a log, rain and wind can't bother them!

eggs

FUN FACT

The carpenter ant queen lays many eggs. When the first ones hatch into babies or **larvae**, she feeds her other eggs to them.

Welcome Worms

Earthworms squirm through rotting logs and forest floors to eat their favorite foods. They chomp on poo and pieces of dead plants and animals.

earthworm

leaf

This earthworm has its mouth full!

Feasting on Poo

Millipedes chew up dead leaves and wood and leave their poo behind. **Microbes** grow on that poo. Those microbes make a very tasty feast for creatures like springtails and mites!

springtail

millipede

Blind and Dangerous

The forest floor is home to many centipedes. Most are blind. But watch out! They are dangerous killers. They kill insects for food by **injecting**, or putting, poison into them.

This centipede is busy eating a spider.

23

Battling Termites

There can be many termites in a rotting log. Soldier termites protect their **colony**, or group, from enemies like ants. Some soldier termites have no eyes. Instead, they have giant heads and long, sharp jaws.

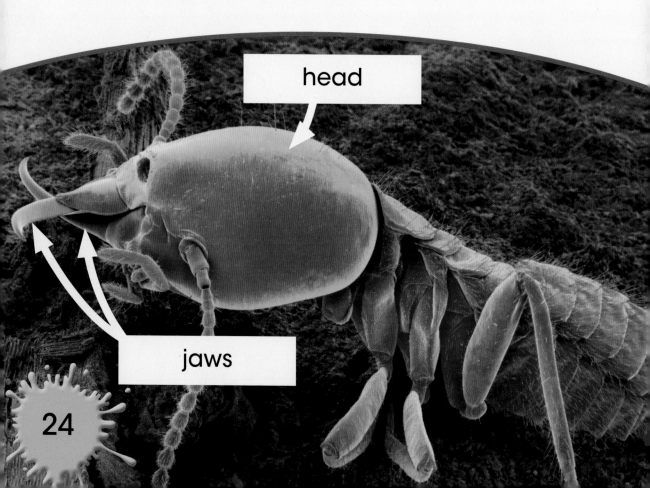

head

jaws

FUN FACT

Soldier termites can be male or female.

FUN FACT

If the **colony** runs low on food, the worker termites eat the soldier termites. They don't fight back – they just give themselves up for lunch!

26

Some soldier termites protect the colony in another way. They shoot poison goo from their foreheads.

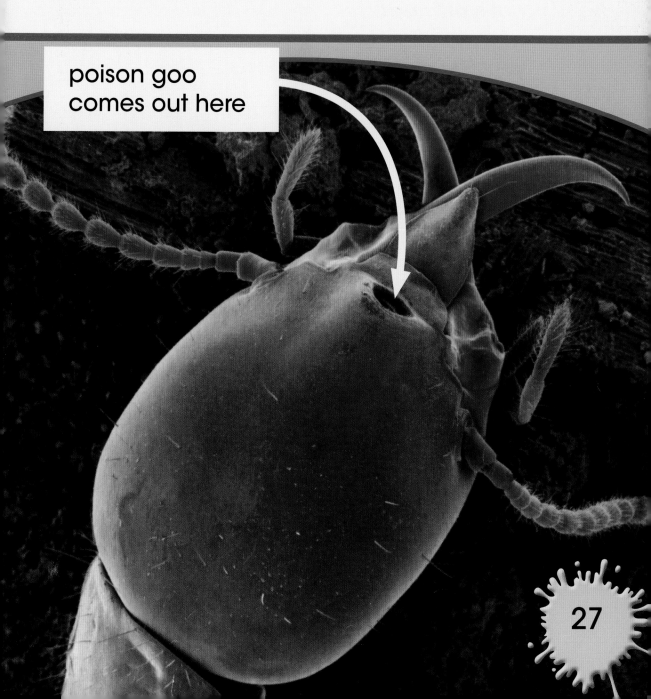

poison goo comes out here

Explore a Rotting Tree

What you need:
- a hand lens
- your eyes

What to do:

1. Find a rotting log in a nearby forest or park.

2. Look around carefully. See how many of these things you can find:

a. an earthworm
b. a beetle
c. an ant
d. a millipede
e. a mushroom
f. a pill bug

a

b

c

d

e

f

29

Glossary

antibiotic substance, like a medicine, that is used to stop illnesses caused by living things such as bacteria or fungus

bacteria type of microbe. Some bacteria can cause illness in people and other animals.

colony large group of animals

digest to break food down inside the body so that it can be used

fungus plant-like living things, similar to mushrooms

habitat place where plants and animals live and grow

inject to put something into something else

larvae the young of some types of insects

microbe tiny living thing that can only be seen under a microscope

molting when an animal sheds its skin or shell and grows a new one

Find Out More

Find out

How do ants hear without ears?

Books to Read

Gaarder-Juntti, Oona. *What Lives in the Forest?* Edina, MN: 2008.

Kalman, Bobbi. *A Forest Habitat.* New York: Crabtree Publishing Company, 2009.

–*Forest Food Chains.* New York: Crabtree Publishing Company, 2004.

Websites

http://ant.edb.miyakyo-u.ac.jp/ INTRODUCTION/Gakken79E/Page_49.html
This Website helps you set up your own study of ants!

http://www.biokids.umich.edu/critters/ Coleoptera/
This Website helps you learn about all kinds of beetles!

http://www.earthlife.net/insects/ants.html
This Website gives you lots of information about ants.

http://www.enchantedlearning.com/biomes/
This Website has illustrations of many forest animals.

Index